MAX E. JAMES

BIRTHDAY BASH

PART 2

J. RYAN HERSEY

Illustrated by Gustavo Mazali

TABLE OF CONTENTS

To my good friend, Britt – may the commute always be long.

FREE DOWNLOAD

In case you downloaded part 2 before reading part 1, join my Kids' Club to get your free copy of the second book in the Max E. James children's series. Type the link below into your browser to get started.

http://eepurl.com/cfcfkj

CHAPTER 1

Let's Get This Party Started!

G-DUDE AND DADDY were carrying something wrapped in a tarp. I wondered what it could be. And what was that rope for?

Daddy tossed the rope over a tree branch. G-Dude caught it on the other side.

Jo-Jo appeared beside me, ready to investigate. We walked toward G-Dude and Daddy.

"What are they doing, Max?" he asked, keeping pace with me.

"I don't know," I said.

As we approached, G-Dude pulled on the rope and the tarp fell away.

A giant head with huge eyes rose into the air. Its

long, pink tongue dangled in the wind while G-Dude tied it off about head height.

"Wow," I said. "Look at that!"

Jo-Jo didn't say anything. He just stared at the papier-mâché masterpiece.

I tapped him on the shoulder.

"That's the coolest piñata I've ever seen," he said.

"Yeah," I said. "That Chihuahua head is almost as big as I am."

Everyone ran up to us as the piñata spun slowly. It seemed to scan the party with its huge bug eyes.

"All right, if we're going to do this, everyone get behind this line," he said, scratching a line in the dirt under the giant Chihuahua head. "I need everyone right here, lined up from smallest to biggest."

He pointed with the stick and the eager line wriggled like a snake as it formed. Mommy handed everyone a plastic bag.

"You may need these," she said.

I worked my way to the front of the line. Not only was it my birthday, but I was also the smallest of the bunch.

"Yay," I said. "I'm first!"

G-Dude spread the blue tarp beneath the piñata. I could actually feel the excitement as I stepped forward.

I marveled at it for a minute. The huge ears made it look just like a real Chihuahua. Its tongue dangled toward the ground—it made a wonderful target.

I grabbed the stick and wound up, but Daddy caught it before I could swing.

"Hold on a second," he said.

He pulled a strip of black cloth from his pocket. "Not without a blindfold. This has to last at least one round."

Reluctantly, I allowed him to tie it around my head. When he finished, I couldn't see a thing.

He spun me around five times and told me to swing. I could hear whispers and giggles from behind me. I took a deep breath and swung with all my might.

CHAPTER 2

Swinging for the Fences

SWISH!

My stick sliced through the air but hit nothing. The crowd giggled as I pulled off the blindfold. The piñata had vanished.

"Behind you," Cody said. He pointed over my shoulder.

"Very funny," I said.

"Okay," Daddy said. "We'll give him another chance since it's his birthday."

He re-tied the blindfold and spun me around again. I tightened my grip and stretched the stick out in front of me. I wiggled it back and forth until I found the piñata. Not going to miss you this time, I thought. I drew back and let it fly.

Swish!

I missed again.

"What!?" I screamed, tearing off the blindfold.

G-Dude greeted me with a smile and pointed up with his eyes. The piñata hung above me, well out of my reach.

"Hey! No fair," I said.

He lowered the piñata back down.

"We're just kidding," Daddy said. "We won't move it again." He put the blindfold back on.

"All right, Max," he said. "Try it now."

I swung as hard as I could. I didn't even wait this time.

Crack!

My hands stung from the vibrating stick.

"There must be a lot of candy in there," Herby said. "It barely moved."

"About twenty pounds by my estimate," said G-Dude.

Jo-Jo was next in line.

"Get ready," he said. "I'm going to whack it."

He swung the stick back and forth as Daddy adjusted the blindfold from behind.

Thwack!

He struck it in the same spot as me – the dent was visible now.

Jacob went next. Then Herby took his turn. Both had solid hits, but didn't do much damage. Cody and Seamus went last. Not only were they the biggest, but they also played baseball.

Cody walked up first and sized up the piñata. He spun it around so that the dent was right in front then Daddy blindfolded him.

Faah-whaap!

A piece of the ear sailed through the air, but no candy fell out.

Everyone giggled and slowly crept toward the tarp.

"Not yet," Daddy said. "Stay behind the line."

Cody handed the stick to Seamus, who looked like he was stepping up to home plate to swing for the fences.

Whack!

Without warning, he struck the piñata so hard that Herby almost jumped out of his skin.

"Okay," Daddy said. "Now everyone gets a second hit."

The line started over and I noticed a small crack on one side. My second attempt convinced a single piece of candy to fall out. I grabbed it, handed the stick to Jo-Jo, and headed to the end of the line.

"Now we're really getting somewhere," Jo-Jo said.

"I can almost taste the candy," Jacob said.

The onslaught continued as piñata pieces continued to fall away. The tongue lay on the ground beneath the twirling head. You could hardly tell it was a Chihuahua anymore. The good news was that the crack had grown.

By the time it was Cody's turn, candy was dribbling out with every hit.

"You got this," Seamus said.

Without hesitation, Cody swung and a bunch of candy fell to the ground.

The kids rushed onto the tarp to retrieve it.

"Wait, wait, wait," Daddy said. "Not yet."

He tried to maintain order, but it was hard to do with all the bubble gum, lollipops, and chocolate bars scattered across the tarp. My mouth watered.

We all knew the next hit would release the sweet treasure. Cody carefully lined up the stick and unloaded with all his might. Instantly, a shower of color exploded before us as the orderly line erupted into chaos.

CHAPTER 3

Candy Doesn't Have a Tax

A SQUEAL PIERCED the air as the avalanche of sweets spread across the tarp.

"Candy!" someone screamed. Daddy jumped out of the way just before we dove into the mound.

I worked my way in and grabbed all the chocolate and bubble gum I could find.

In what seemed like seconds, the heaping pile was reduced to a few empty wrappers and broken pieces.

"Wow," Herby said, lifting his bulging bag. "That's a lot of candy."

Jo-Jo frantically unwrapped piece after piece and devoured chocolate bars and gummy treats. Chocolate dripped from the corners of his mouth as he stuffed them in.

"Easy," Jacob said. "You don't want to get a stomach ache."

Over Jo-Jo's shoulder I noticed Daddy and the other grown-ups walking into the yard carrying plastic grocery bags. I was just about to call after them when I heard Cody yell, "Candy tax!"

Seamus and Cody were working their way through the party, going through everyone's bag.

"Candy tax?" Herby asked. "What are you two blabbing about now?"

Cody grinned. "We did most of the work, so we should get most of the candy."

Seamus nodded in agreement. "It's our tax for breaking it. If it wasn't for us, you wouldn't have anything."

I scanned the yard for some grown-up support, but there was none to be found. They were still scattering grocery bags throughout the backyard. We'd have to face this on our own.

I looked back at Cody.

"You don't get a candy tax," I said. "We all helped bust the piñata."

"Candy tax!" Cody said, leaning in closer to me.

"I got your tax right here," I said.

I reached into my bag, pulled out a wrapper, and dropped it in his hand. I don't think he liked that because he shoved his hand into my bag and pawed through it. I grabbed his wrist with both hands and sank to the ground.

Jo-Jo pounced on his legs.

"Oh, no you don't," he said, wrapping around him like an octopus. "You're not getting a single piece of his candy."

Cody almost had his hand free when Mommy walked by.

"Um," she said, "what are you boys doing?"

"They're taxing our candy!" I screamed.

Cody looked up and smiled.

"I was just trying to share with the birthday boy," he said.

"Sure, Cody," she said. "Let him go. There was twenty pounds of candy in that piñata – plenty for everyone."

He let go then he smiled at me with a twinkle in his eyes. Something told me that this wasn't over yet.

I looked him dead in the eye, took a step forward, and tilted my head to one side.

Just as I was about to open my mouth, Daddy and the other grown-ups appeared. Their faces glistened in the sun.

"Man," Daddy said. "That was hard work."

"What are you talking about?" I asked.

Daddy pointed at the yard, which was littered with bulging grocery bags.

Everyone looked out across the sea of bags. Nobody knew quite what to say, because we didn't know what we were looking at.

"What's so great about bags?" I asked.

"Oh, my son," he said. "It's not the bags. It's what's in them."

CHAPTER 4

What's in the Bags?

"WHAT'S IN THE bags?" I asked.

"Okay, kids," Daddy said, ignoring me. "Go get your bathing suits on."

Everyone scattered but me.

"You too, Max," he said. "You don't want to miss this."

I scowled and ran into the house. Jo-Jo, Herby, and Jacob were already piled in my room and furiously changing into their suits.

My mind raced as we changed in silence. It could be squirt guns, I thought. Maybe sprinklers? No, not in bags. How would they sprinkle?

We spilled out the door onto the deck where Seamus and Cody were already waiting.

"Okay," Daddy said. "Is everyone here?"

"Yes!" we screamed.

"All right then," he said. "Take a seat and I'll explain the rules." He pointed to the steps leading to the deck.

We looked out across the backyard at the lumpy grocery bags. Their sides bulged like sacks of potatoes.

I elbowed Herby. "Do you see colors? It looks like they're filled with something colorful."

I raised my hand.

"Excuse me," I said.

"Yes, Max."

"What's in the bags?"

"Yeah!" everyone screamed. "Tell us!"

Daddy smiled as he revealed a perfect globe. He held it high above his head and dropped it. The sun sparkled through its clear blue skin just before it exploded at his feet.

"Water balloons!" he screamed.

Everybody jumped to their feet and cheered. We started down the stairs, but Daddy stopped us.

"Whoa, whoa, whoa," he said. "Rules first."

We could barely contain ourselves, like a dam ready to overflow.

"Who wants to throw water balloons?" he shouted.

Everyone screamed, "I do!"

"Great," he said. "Then you're also willing to get hit. Right?"

"Yeah!" we all screamed.

"Okay," he said. "Don't pick up the bags." Daddy's eyes shifted to Cody and Seamus. "And no ganging up."

We all nodded, but out of the corner of my eye I caught Cody winking at Seamus.

I stuck my tongue out at Cody. He just smiled and blew me a kiss.

"Does anybody have any questions?" Daddy asked.

"No!" everyone yelled.

"Well," he said. "Why are you guys still sitting around?"

CHAPTER 5

Double Teamed

WE WERE OFF like a shot sprinting toward the bags. The first one I opened was filled with water balloons of all different colors. I grabbed a few and looked for my first victim.

"Look out!" Jo-Jo said. I turned to look and felt a balloon whiz past my head before splashing on the ground beside me.

"Whoa," I said. "That was close. Who threw that?"

It was no use. A rainbow of water balloons littered the sky as kids ran in all directions. I bent down to reload and was hit in the stomach.

"Ugh," I said. "These things are not as soft as they look."

"I know," Jo-Jo said. He pulled up his shirt to reveal a red splotch.

Seamus and Cody were doubled over with laughter, pointing at us.

"Direct hit," I heard Cody say.

"Let's get them!" Jo-Jo said.

Herby and Jacob ran by and I grabbed them.

"You guys want to help us get Cody and Seamus?"

They nodded.

"Those two have it coming," Jacob said.

We grabbed as many water balloons as we could carry and ran in their direction. Cody spotted us and signaled Seamus.

They began firing and balloons exploded all around us as we ran.

A pink balloon whooshed by my head, then I took one on the knee. I turned to see Herby get blasted in the chest. He dropped every balloon he was carrying.

One slammed directly into Jo-Jo's stomach and he went down too.

"Man down! Man down!" Jacob cried as he stopped to assist the fallen.

Now he was a sitting duck and our attackers knew it. They unleashed a flurry of strikes as fast as they could throw. Jo-Jo and Jacob never had a chance.

It was up to me now. I ran through the barrage, clutching four water balloons. They jiggled as I dodged throws. It was only when I reached them that I realized my back-up was gone. I turned to see my posse running in the opposite direction. Surely they would return with reinforcements. I just had to hold my ground until then.

I stopped within firing range. Cody walked closer.

"Okay, Max," he said. "Take your best shot."

"Yeah," Seamus said. He leaned forward and pointed to his chin.

I lobbed one at Cody. He leaned in just before it connected. It breezed past his cheek and burst on the ground. The next one did the same.

Cody laughed and Seamus stepped forward.

"Two left," Seamus said. "Better make them count."

I threw them both as hard as I could, but they fell short and splashed at his feet. His grin grew as Cody handed him a bag of balloons.

"Hey," I said, looking around for the nearest place to reload. "That's against the rules!"

"We're going to make an exception for you," Cody said.

I tried to run, but stumbled and crashed to the

ground. I managed to roll onto my back, but they were upon me.

All I could see were their smiling faces as the sun shone through the water balloons they held.

"Well, well, well," Seamus said. "What do we have here?"

"I don't know," Cody said. "Looks like someone in trouble to me."

My heart pounded and a lump grew in my throat – they were not going to go easy on me.

Cody dropped one onto my forehead. The cool water drenched my head and some even got up my nose. It made me cough.

"Oh, I'm sorry," Cody said. "I must have dropped that one. I'm so clumsy."

Seamus released one onto my chest next. He laughed as it exploded and soaked my shirt.

"Hey!" I said, propping myself up on my elbows. "This isn't fair. It's two against one and I don't have any ammo."

I scanned the yard for my cavalry, but I was alone.

"You're right," Cody said. "We'll give you a head start."

Before I had time to react, they started counting.

"One. Two!" they shouted and unloaded water balloons on me as I tried to crawl away.

I tried to duck and cover, but they were coming too fast. Colors rained down on my head and
back. It lasted for what seemed like forever, then,
as quick as it began, it was over.

"Out of water balloons," Seamus said.

And just like that, they disappeared.

I lay in a puddle of muddy water and pride. I
rolled onto my back and leaned my head into the
slop. That's when I saw a shadow.

"Wow," Jo-Jo said. "They really got you."

I looked up. Herby and Jacob were standing beside Jo-Jo.

"Thanks a lot, guys," I said. "Where were you?"

"We went to reload and got ambushed by your dad," Jo-Jo said.

"He throws hard," Herby said, rubbing his back.

"Yeah," Jacob said. "We got back as quick as we could, but it was too late."

They pulled me up from the mud.

"Boy," Jacob said. "There isn't a dry spot on you."

"Thanks for noticing," I said as we walked to the next bag of balloons. "They have to pay."

"Hey. "Where are Seamus and Cody going?" Jo-Jo asked.

There was a row of bushes at the back of the yard. Cody and Seamus ducked behind them.

"They're stashing water balloons," I said. "That's cheating."

We walked toward them.

"Whoa," Herby cried, crashing to the ground.

We lifted him up. There was something tangled around his feet.

"Dumb piñata rope," he said, kicking it off.

I smiled and picked it up.

"Bring it in boys," I said. "It's payback time."

Chapter 6

Payback Time

I TORE THE last bit of piñata from the rope and snapped it taught.

"All right," I said. "Here's what we're going to do."

They huddled around and I explained my plan. It was a dangerous mission, but smiles grew wide on their faces as they listened carefully.

"Okay," I said as I coiled the rope and put it in the rear of my pants. "Ready?"

They nodded.

"Only one thing left to decide," I said. "Who's the bait?"

They all looked down at their feet and shuffled them in the grass.

"I'll do it," Jo-Jo said and stepped forward.

"You're a good man," I said. "You won't be forgotten."

I handed him two plump water balloons. Jo-Jo nodded and smiled.

I turned to Herby and Jacob who each had two full bags of water balloons.

"Are you guys ready?" I asked.

"Ready as I'll ever be," Herby said.

"Yup," Jacob said.

We stepped into the open at the perfect time. Seamus and Cody were in the middle of a battle with Daddy and G-Dude, so they didn't see us creep up from behind.

"Now's our chance," I said. "Go, Jo-Jo!"

He took off toward Seamus at full speed. The water balloons jiggled in his hands. Seamus turned back toward the bushes and Jo-Jo slammed a pink water balloon into his face. The blast drenched him instantly. Before he could react, Jo-Jo chucked another one. It hit him square in the chest.

"Take that!" he screamed and sped away.

Seamus grabbed a bag of balloons and took off after him.

Luckily for us, Cody didn't see the exchange and his back was still to us. Jacob and Herby attacked as he ducked behind the bushes to reload.

Cody was so caught up with them, he didn't notice

me slip behind the other side of the bushes. I pulled the rope from my pants and crawled toward him.

I slipped the rope around his feet and screamed, "Get him!"

Jacob and Herby tackled Cody and pinned him to the ground. I furiously wrapped the rope around his legs as he lay thrashing, and tied his feet together with my very best knot.

"You guys better let me go," he said. "Or else."

"Or else what?" Herby said. "Looks like you aren't going anywhere to me."

"Yeah," Jacob said. "We got you now!"

We stood above him admiring our handiwork as he struggled to free his legs.

"Don't worry, Cody," I whispered, reaching into the bag. "I triple-knotted it."

We pelted him with water balloons. They exploded all over him.

Cody couldn't decide whether to cover his face or untie the rope. He flailed his arms from his face to his feet and back again.

"Take that!" I shouted. "How do you like it?"

Herby and Jacob continued throwing, and the puddle surrounding Cody grew. That's when I saw a blur of color out of the corner of my eye – it was Jo-Jo! He sprinted by and smashed a balloon right into Cody's face with great delight.

"Time to get moving, guys," he said between deep breaths. "Seamus is hot on my tail."

We looked up and saw him running toward us, lobbing balloons as he approached.

"Let him go," he yelled. "Get off of him!"

Laughing with delight, we all got up and ran. As I turned, I slammed into something and fell backwards. It was Daddy. I looked up at his scowling face.

CHAPTER 7

Ice Cream and Cake

I BOUNCED OFF his legs and fell to the ground.

"I can explain," I said, grinning.

"I'm sure you can," he said.

I opened my mouth to speak and a water balloon slammed into my back. The explosion sprayed Daddy's shirt.

"Ouch!" I said, rubbing my back.

Seamus stood behind me with another balloon locked and loaded.

"How do you like it?" he asked.

Daddy leaned to one side of us to get a better look at the soggy boy lumped on the ground.

Cody was still trying to untie his feet.

"They did it first!" I screamed.

Daddy looked at Cody.

"Is that true?"

"It is," Jo-Jo said, joining the group. "They ganged up on Max."

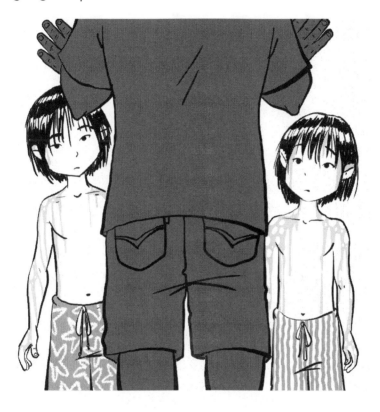

"Cody?" he asked again.

"Well, yes," he said, "but we were just having fun."

"You bombarded me!" I screamed.

"We gave you a head start," Cody said, now standing.

I frowned and felt my cheeks getting hot. "Two seconds isn't a head start!"

"All of you broke my rules," Daddy said. "Including you guys." He pointed to Herby, Jacob, and Jo-Jo, who were slinking away.

"True," Seamus said. "But it was all in good fun and nobody got hurt. Right, Max?"

"I guess so," I said.

Cody was soaked from head to toe. He lifted his shirt to reveal a bunch of welts on his stomach.

"I'd say it was pretty even," he said. He put his hand on my shoulder and patted me on the back. "I can appreciate a good water balloon strike."

"Well," Daddy said, "Did you have fun?"

"Yes!" we all yelled.

"I guess we can let it go," he said. "But no more ganging up on people. Now you boys pick up the empty bags."

We all took off through the yard and grabbed bags as we went. We threw any straggling water balloons we found.

Mommy appeared on the deck minutes later with a pile of towels. "Dry off and change your clothes. Then we'll have ice cream and cake."

"Oh no," I said. In all the fun, I had forgotten

my wish. My heart sank a little, but there was no time for that. I had one more chance.

I sprinted into the house to change. My friends followed and were back outside in a flash.

On our way out, I noticed the pile of birthday presents in the living room.

"I have to make this one count," I said as we walked onto the deck.

Jo-Jo heard me muttering to myself. "Make what count?" he asked.

"My birthday wish," I said. "The candles are my last shot and I have to make them count. One breath, I have to do it in one breath."

CHAPTER 8

That Takes Care of You

MOMMY UNVEILED THE cake and placed seven candles around the face of the Chihuahua.

"Careful of the eyes, Mommy!" I said.

She lit each one as I reached for the corner of the cake.

"Don't touch that cake, Max. Not until we sing 'Happy Birthday' and even then don't stick your fingers in it."

I batted my eyes and lowered my hand. I took a huge breath in. The frosting smelled wonderful.

"Everyone gather round," Mommy said.

We stepped closer.

"One. Two. Three," she said and then raised her arms and conducted the group.

The crowd erupted with the lyrics of "Happy Birthday" as the candles flickered.

"Happy birthday to you, cha, cha, cha. Happy birthday to you, cha, cha, cha," echoed through the yard.

The singing faded into the background as I focused on the candles. I had to harness all my wishing power in one giant blow. If I could extinguish them in a single breath, maybe my wish would come true. All I could think of was a cute little Chihuahua. That was all I wanted.

I snapped back to the moment. They were on the last verse, so I took a huge breath. As I inhaled, my lungs burned and felt as if they would burst, like an over-filled balloon. I took my last sip of air, just as the final note trailed off.

"Blow out your candles, Max," someone yelled.

I blew so hard I thought the candles might fly off the cake. Luckily that didn't happen. All that was left were trails of smoke where the flames had been.

Everyone cheered.

I smiled and started to take a bow when I noticed a candle still smoldering. I put my hands on my knees and leaned in for a closer look. What was that? I watched in amazement as a flame sprouted from the thin trail of smoke. Then another flame appeared. Then another, until all seven candles were ablaze.

"What?!" I said. "I just blew you out!"

Laughter swept through the crowd and Mommy and Daddy smiled.

"You'll just have to blow them out again," Daddy said.

My stomach felt sick. I didn't know how this

unfortunate event would affect my wish. I had worked so hard and now it was slipping away.

I took another huge breath and blew them out again.

"There," I said. "Now you're out."

Again the candles flickered back to a flame. This couldn't be happening.

"Trick candles?!" I said. "No fair!"

I snatched them off the cake and threw them on the ground. I crushed each one with the heel of my foot, leaving a wax smear on the deck.

"Let's see you come back from that!" I said, smiling.

Everyone roared with laughter.

"Cut the cake already," Cody said.

"I want that piece," Jo-Jo shouted.

"Can I have an ear?" Herby asked.

"An eye for me," Jacob said. "May I please have an eye?"

Mommy portioned out the cake to the hungry mob and Daddy scooped the ice cream. We moved inside with our full plates and sat in a circle around the pile of presents.

"Okay, everyone," Mommy said. "It's present time!"

I tore through the first gift's wrapping paper as everyone watched.

"Hmm," I said, clutching the box. "How can it breathe in there?"

I ripped off the paper and found a box of building blocks.

"Oh," I said. "I like blocks and love to build stuff. Thanks."

I grabbed the next present – it was an envelope.

"Too small," I said and ripped it open. "A gift card! Sweet."

The crowd crept closer with each gift I unwrapped. Fingers, sticky with ice cream and cake, reached for their chance to rip a piece of wrapping paper. There's something about presents that everyone loves. Before I knew it everyone started tearing edges of the gifts I picked up. The flurry of paper ripping left a pile of unwrapped gifts in the center of the floor. There were blocks, gift cards, puzzles, action figures, and stuffed animals, but no Chihuahua.

"Happy Birthday, Max!" everyone shouted. I stood before the pile of shredded paper and gifts.

"Thank you," I said, forcing a smile.

I was thankful and appreciated all the gifts, but

I didn't get the one thing I truly wanted and had wished so hard for.

I sat back down and sank deep into the couch to finish my ice cream and cake.

"What's the matter, Max?" Jo-Jo asked.

"I just don't understand," I said softly. "I tried so hard this year and that's all I've really ever wanted."

"It had to be those trick candles," he said. "I

don't know how to score that one. It might have counted against you."

"Yeah," I said. "I guess there's always next year."

Bing-Bong! Bing-Bong!

My heart raced as the sound of the doorbell pierced the room.

I caught Mommy's gaze and my heart fluttered. She smiled warmly.

"I wonder who that could be," she said.

I dropped my plate and sprinted for the door.

CHAPTER 9

Really and Truly Over

I COULD HARDLY believe it. My heart pumped and pumped as I ran for the door.

Bing-bong! Bing-bong!

"My wish," I said under my breath. "It has to be my wish!"

Jo-Jo sprang up and joined me.

I flung the door open with such force it slammed into the wall with a thud. I didn't have time to care; I had to see what was on the other side.

My face crumbled as the figure at the door became clear. Jo-Jo's face dropped even further and we stood, mouths open.

"Happy Birthday, Max," Jo-Jo's Mom said.

"Oh," I said. "Hello, Jo-Jo's Mom. And thank you."

Jo-Jo ran back into the house, away from his mom.

"Wow," she said. "You guys sure know how to make a lady feel wanted."

I smiled.

"Hello, Mary," Mommy called from behind me. "Come on in, we're just wrapping up."

She chatted with Mommy about the party while Jo-Jo and I gathered his things.

"Thanks for coming over," I said. "I had a great time."

"Me too," he said. "This was the best party ever! I can't wait until next year."

"What was your favorite part?

"Definitely the water balloon fight," he said. "It was epic."

"You're right about that," I said.

"I'm sorry you didn't get your wish. Maybe next year."

"I guess so," I said. "It was still a pretty great day. It just wasn't in the cards apparently."

"See you later, Max."

And with that, Jo-Jo was gone.

The doorbell continued to ring throughout the afternoon. Each time, another friend left until all that remained was wrapping paper, dirty plates, and a few pieces of piñata candy that nobody wanted.

"All right, everyone," Mommy said. "Time to clean up."

"But it's my birthday," I said. "I don't have to, right?"

"Sorry," Mommy said. "It goes along with hosting a party. Please start with the backyard."

"Come on," Cody said. "Wasn't the party worth it?"

"Yes, but I didn't get what I wished for," I said.

"I know you really wanted a Chihuahua," Mommy said. "But that's a big responsibility."

"It's the only thing I've wished for since I can remember," I said. "Every birthday and Christmas, it's the same wish."

We made our way to the backyard to pick up any trash that had missed the can.

"You can't win them all," Cody said.

"Hey, at least you got some pretty cool stuff." he said.

"I sure did."

"What was your favorite?" he asked.

"Probably the robot Chihuahua," I answered. "That's the closest thing to a real dog."

"Cool," he said. "By the way, what did you get from Mommy and Daddy?"

I sat puzzled for a minute, but couldn't put my finger on it.

"I have no idea," I said as a sparkle returned to my eye. "Let's go find out."

We dashed back to the house.

"We finished the trash," Cody said.

Mommy, Daddy, Hunny-G, and G-Dude were all sitting at the kitchen table relaxing.

"Mommy! Daddy!" I said. "What'd you get me for my birthday?"

Daddy looked blankly at me and Mommy smiled.

"What do you mean, Max?" Mommy said.

"My birthday present," I said. "Where is it?"

Mommy chuckled. "What do you think this birthday party was? I heard you say it was the best party ever."

"What?!" I screamed. "The party was my present?!"

"Yes, son," Daddy said, frowning. "The party."

My heart sunk. This was the first time I realized that it was truly over. My wish had not come true.

"Now," Mommy said. "I have one more thing I need you to do."

I couldn't speak, so I just looked up at her as my eyes began to fill with tears.

"Empty the waste-paper baskets in the

bathrooms," Mommy said. "They're always full after a party."

All the happiness drained right out of me. I was so beaten I couldn't even complain.

"I got this one," Cody said and headed for the hallway bathroom.

"Max, you can go empty my bathroom," Daddy said.

I slumped down the hall to their room. I opened the door and felt a cool rush of air as I walked in. The blinds were closed and it was dark. I thought it would make a nice place to cry later. I headed for the bathroom door, which was also closed.

That's funny, I thought. It's usually open. My eyes began to fill with tears as I reached for the door-knob.

When I opened the door, I couldn't believe my eyes. I rubbed them and burst into tears.

Sitting before me, curled up in a ball, was a little white Chihuahua puppy. It was fast asleep on a pillow laid on the bathroom floor.

Tears rolled down my cheeks. I scooped up the sleepy puppy. Its perfect tiny paws stretched as it yawned. She licked the salty tears from my cheeks with her little pink tongue.

I turned to leave the bathroom and saw everyone peering through the doorway with huge smiles
on their faces.

"Happy Birthday, Max," they cheered.

I stood speechless, holding my birthday wish.
All I could manage was a single sentence whis-
pered in my puppy's ear: "I think I'll name you
Birthday Miracle."

FROM THE AUTHOR

If you enjoyed this book, please leave an honest review. Word-of-mouth is truly powerful, and your words will make a huge difference. Thank you.

As you read this, I'm writing the next Max E. James adventure. For updates on new releases, promotions, and other great children's book recommendations, join my Kids' Club at:

http://www.maxejames.com/kids-club/

DON'T FORGET YOUR FREE DOWNLOAD

In case you missed it, be sure to pick it up for free!
Type the link below into your browser to get started.
http://eepurl.com/cfcfkj

About the Author

J. Ryan Hersey is a devoted father and husband who lives in beautiful Hampton Roads, Virginia. His stories are inspired by the adventures he shares with his wife and two boys. He is author of the Max E. James children's series. To find out more or connect with him directly, visit his website at:

http://www.maxejames.com

About the Illustrator

Gustavo Mazali lives with his family in beautiful Buenos Aires, Argentina. Having drawn all his life, Gustavo has developed the unique ability to capture the essence of children in his art. You can view his portfolio at:

http://www.mazali.com

About the Editor

Amy Betz founded Tiny Tales Editing after working as a children's book editor at several major publishing houses. She lives with her family in Bethel, Connecticut. You can learn more about Amy at:

http://www.tinytalesediting.com

ALL TITLES

Beach Bound
Birthday Bash: Part 1
Birthday Bash: Part 2
Fishing Fever
Winter Wipeout
Crash Course

Made in the USA
Lexington, KY
29 November 2019

57870666R00036